# Scalping is fun!

I0468219

## Part 4: Trading is flow business

**Heikin Ashi Trader**

# Table of Contents

# 1. Only trade when it's fun

A successful trader does not go into the casino. He is the casino. More specifically: A successful trader is playing the cards on his own terms. He decides himself, how and when he is trading and especially when he does not trades. Knowing when to stay out of the market is one of the crucial benefits that a trader can have against "the market".

It is only natural that a beginning trader initially spends a lot of time to find a suitable strategy. Much less or no time he invests to find out when this new strategy works best.

I want in this fourth part of the series "scalping is fun" especially go into the right time to trade.

Our time is precious. We should as a trader therefore put every effort only to go to the stock market, if the conditions for us are optimal. In the hours in which this is not the case, we should dedicate ourselves better to other things.

Above all, we should try to prevent from the so-called trading out of boredom. This is a condition in which the trader clearly feels that nothing is to pick up in this phase of the market. Yet, he sits in front of his monitor and observes the market with a sleeping eye. Worse. From time to time he makes a trade out of sheer boredom, even if nothing comes out of it.

It is the precursor to addiction-trading. Just as almost anything can be an addiction, trading too can turn into a true addiction.

I myself have certainly recognized such traits in me in my novice years. I was fascinated by the stock market and by this opportunity so to speak to make money out of nothing. I even stayed up at night to trade the asian markets even though I had a 16-hour day in European trading and the US trading in the bones. I think, the fact that nothing good has come out of this in the long run, should be clear.

This book is not written for the traders who are at risk here. It wants to show especially scalper the way when the "action" takes place in the markets. And it should be an encouragement, to pick up at these times even the most out of the market.

------------------------------------

So that you can live out your enthusiasm at the right time, it is therefore important that you take pleasure in trading at the times where it is possible. The risk of addiction is not yet completely eliminated, but you have at least abated. Perhaps is it for you then it easier to connect the computer and to pursue other things.

Fun at the right time is an effective means against the risk of trading and Over of trading out of boredom for me.

You will then have the most success if your strategy blends well with the market conditions, so that you have the probabilities in your advantage. This can be for example a trend trader something quite different from a scalper.

Surely this knowledge has to do with "experience", but thank God, the learning curve is faster than with any other trading strategies with a scalper because of the many trades.

You now have time to lose no time and should make your experience as soon as possible, so that you exceed the profitability threshold.

Experienced traders know, "when to sit on Their Hands," as expressing the Americans. Sitting on your hands means that you need to be a good observer of the stockmarket first.

You need to find out on the basis of many hours "chart Reading", when the moment has come that you can get involved and when you retire better. Boss one day this ability, then you definitely arrived in the Master game.

Also in stock exchange trading, it is important that you use your time intelligently and efficiently. The pauses between the individual trading sessions come while greater importance.

This applies both for lunch on the trade date itself, as well as occasional breaks during the year. In the next chapter I will enumerate a whole series of events that you better avoid. It usually is not worth it to trade at these times.

Moreover, I would also my vacation planning act accordingly. A fellow trader told me that he had achieved in the whole month of August, no gains. Worse: He had losses. He wanted to trade even though he knew that many bankers, who are involved in currency trading, in August are on vacation. Of course, the currency trading also takes place at this time, but it had used him nothing. "I would be better myself four weeks went on holiday," he told me. It would have been much cheaper.

# 2. When not to trade

Knowing in advance when you should not trade saves you quite a lot of unnecessary and often unproductive hours before the PC. Here are the most important times when you should better avoid trading.

**Bank holidays.** These are particularly important for forex traders. The banks are the largest participants in the Forex. If the bankers have a holiday, the trading volume is greatly reduced. On these days you will often experience lethargic markets or markets with sudden erratic movements. The familiar patterns of your market at these times you are looking in vain.

This is particularly true for bank holidays in the UK and in the US, who are the main centers of the Forex markets. But of course, the rule also applies to holidays in the other major currency areas. If the public holiday is in Australia, then you better avoid the Australian dollar. Is it in Japan, then do not trade the yen, etc.

**Friday afternoon.** Many bankers and traders of hedge funds stop trading on Friday afternoon for the weekend. Mostly they close their positions before the weekend, which is done also by most private traders.

The reason is the so-called weekend gap. This is a price gap that occurs between the closing price on Friday night and the opening on Sunday evening in the Forex market (in the futures markets mostly 08.00 EST or GMT).

**Note:** Hereinafter I will use **EST** (Eastern Standard Time, New York) for American Traders and **GMT** (Greenwich Mean Time) for UK Traders.

This gap is often insignificant, but in some cases it can be huge, especially if there has been an important event or important news came out on the weekend. It might be that elections have taken place, or any other political decisions (think of the Greek crisis). However, it may also be unforeseen events such as earthquakes (Japan!) Or terrorist attacks.

Trading activity on Friday afternoon often slows down accordingly and the markets are more difficult to trade. I myself trade rarely on Friday afternoon, if ever.

**Market close and market-opening**. The final minutes of each trading day are to avoid just as the opening minutes. This is especially true in regulated exchanges such as stock markets and futures markets. Keep in mind that at the end of the day many day traders close their positions. At the end of the trading day liquidity can often be horrible bad. The order book is thin and causes bigger spreads, slippage, and sometimes unexpected movements.

The first minutes of **Monday morning** you should not trade either. The traders who have closed their positions on Friday, open them again on monday morning. That can also cause unexpected movements sometimes.

**Winter and summer holidays**. As already said, if the bankers are on vacation, you'd better do the same. The volume of transactions of the large trading houses drops noticeably during this period.

**Asian Markets**. Even though I have traded the Asian markets myself once, I recommend not to do it. If you are not exactly specializing in Japanese equities you should better preserve your night's rest.

There are always some enthusiasts who want to trade the Hang Seng Futures. But honestly, do the European and American markets not offer enough opportunities? The liquidity in asiatic currency trading is by no means comparable to the European and American session.

Last but not least: the hours **before the release of important economic news**. The calendar tells you when important or even very important economic data will be published. Especially the participants on the forex are waiting for these data. For the calendar that I use visit: www.forexfactory.com.

### Figure 1: Calendar of wednesday, october 14, 2015

| 10:30am | GBP | | Average Earnings Index 3m/y |
| | GBP | | Claimant Count Change |
| | GBP | | Unemployment Rate |
| 11:00am | CHF | | ZEW Economic Expectations |
| | EUR | | Industrial Production m/m |
| 2:30pm | USD | | Core Retail Sales m/m |
| | USD | | PPI m/m |
| | USD | | Retail Sales m/m |

As an example you see here the calendar of Wednesday, 14 October 2015th. On the Forex Factory site pay attention to the color of the small factory symbols next to the description of the message. Is the color yellow or orange, the news usually has little impact on the price action. If the factory-symbol is colored red however, this news is important.

On this day there were basically two important events. At 09.30 GMT, there was the Average Earnings Index in the UK. The publication of this number, of course, had importance for the traders who are trading the British pound.

At 08.30 EST (13.30 GMT) then the Retail Sales from the United States were expected. This is also an important economic data. Let's watch the EUR/USD before and after the release:

## Figure 2: EUR/USD on 14 October 2015, 2-minute chart Heikin Ashi

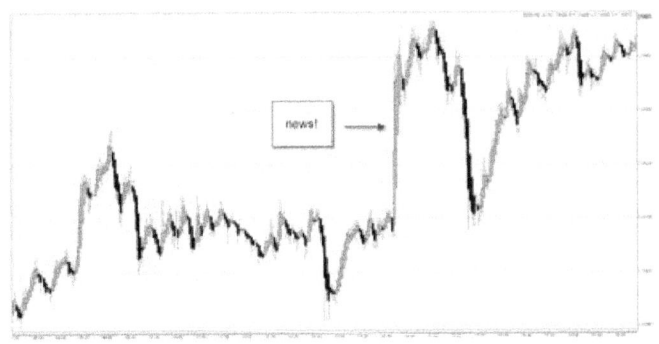

In EUR/USD there was on 14 October basically just one important event and that was precisely the publication of the retail sales at 08.30 EST (13.30 GMT) Before that there was only at 09.00 GMT during the London Open a small jump in the euro. But from 10.00 GMT until 13.30 GMT, the pair ran mainly sideways in a range of less than 10 pips. It is clear that the market players were waiting for the data from 08.30 EST (13.30 GMT).

Such a range is hard to scalp unless you are a specialist in range markets. Basically, one could confidently skip trading till 08.30 EST (13.30 GMT). Only after the publication of the Retail Sales the action came into the market.

## Figure 3: EUR/USD on October 22, 2015 2-minute chart

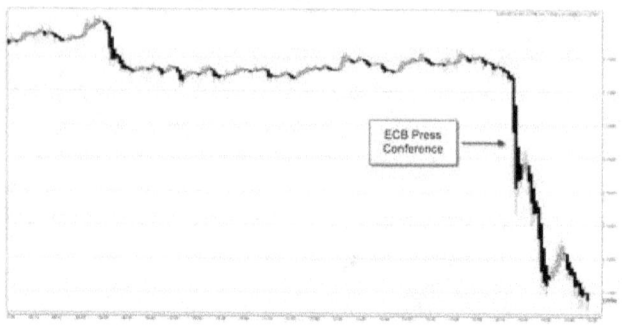

Also Figure 3 leaves nothing left to be desired in clarity. On October 22, the traders were waiting for the interest rate decision of the European Central Bank at 07.45 EST (12.45 GMT). There was hardly any movement in the EUR/USD in the hours before the interest rate decision.

It is also interesting that the market barely moved at the announcement of the interest rate decision at 07.45 EST. This changed dramatically at 08.30 EST (13.30 GMT) as the president of the ECB Mario Draghi appeared in front of the the cameras and the ECB press conference began. The action began, moreover, already at 08.29 EST (13.29 GMT), as if the actors could hardly wait.

**What are the key figures?**

- Figures from the US
- After that, figures from the EU, Germany and the UK
- Figures from Canada, Australia, Japan, New Zealand and Switzerland for the respective currencies

**What numbers have the greatest impact?**

- **Monetary policy**. All important communications or publications along with press conferences of the main central banks

- **Labor market data**: current unemployment rate in Germany and the NFP (Nonfarm payrolls, the first Friday of the month at 08.30 EST (13.30 GMT) in the US.
- **Leading Indicators**: in Germany, the Ifo Business Climate Index. In the US: ISM
  purchasing managers' index
- **Consumer confidence**
- **Gross Domestic Product (GDP)**: important for any large currency area
- **Consumer Price Index** (CPI: Topic: Inflation!)
- **Producer Price Index** (PPI)

You will need a little to study the economic calendar for a while, if you want to trade. It is crucial that you understand that the expectations of market participants are especially important in the forex market. These are often already anticipated in the market in the days prior to the publication. Prior to the publication itself, it is mostly calm.

When the figures are published this expectation is then either confirmed or disappointed. The reaction of the market mostly comes immediately. However, how the market players will respond to a number that is not in the expectation that is difficult to predict. As a scalper, you should try to respond very flexibly without preconception to the buying and selling waves. Trade what you see!

Also study the behavior of market participants in the hours before the release and in the hours afterwards. Many times you will see that the volatility decreases strongly before the publication. After publication, volatility can get quite wild.

# 3. The best trading hours

## A. For Forex Traders

Unlike most other markets, foreign exchange trading is running around the clock. So you can trade all week twenty-four hours and that starting on Sunday evening at 17.00 EST (22.00 GMT) to Friday evening 17.00 EST (22.00 GMT).

The foreign exchange market is not a regular market like the stock market, but a decentralized market with a few trading centers. The main ones are London, New York, Tokyo and Sydney. The "trading day" in currency trading consist therefore of several trading sessions: the European session, the American session and the Asian session.

### Figure 4: Forex Sessions

| Forex Market Center | Time Zone | Opens<br>Europe/Berlin | Closes<br>Europe/Berlin | Status |
|---|---|---|---|---|
| Frankfurt<br>Germany | Europe/Berlin | 08:00 AM<br>06-October-2015 | 04:00 PM<br>06-October-2015 | Open |
| London<br>Great Britain | Europe/London | 09:00 AM<br>06-October-2015 | 05:00 PM<br>06-October-2015 | Open |
| New York<br>United States | America/New York | 02:00 PM<br>06-October-2015 | 10:00 PM<br>06-October-2015 | Closed |
| Sydney<br>Australia | Australia/Sydney | 11:00 PM<br>06-October-2015 | 07:00 AM<br>07-October-2015 | Closed |
| Tokyo<br>Japan | Asia/Tokyo | 01:00 AM<br>07-October-2015 | 09:00 AM<br>07-October-2015 | Closed |

The fascinating thing about Forex is thus that trading goes once around the planet within 24 hours. When traders in Tokyo finish their trading session London traders take over. At 08.00 EST (13.00 GMT) American traders come into the market. Then there is till 11.00 EST (16.00 GMT) an important overlap between these two commercial centers, which is why at this time often the highest volatility is observed (see Figure 4).

After 11.00 EST (16.00 GMT) volatility decreases noticeably. When New York traders are finished with their day's work, the session in Sydney starts again.

**Figure 5: Average volatility EUR/USD per hour (UK)**

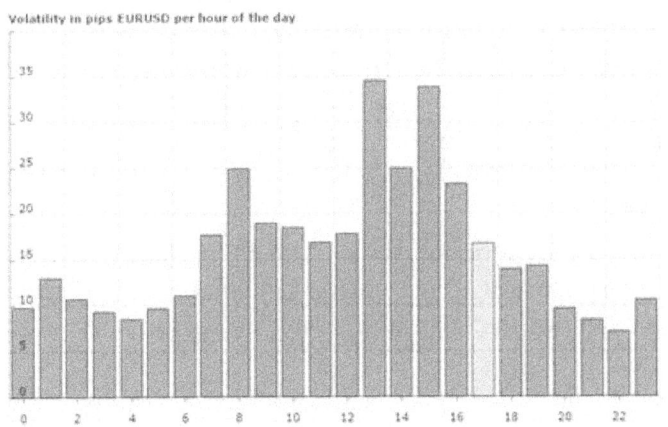

Source: www.mataf.net

Figure 5 illustrates the importance of the sessions very well. Clearly visible is the low volatility during the Asian trade (the extreme left and right side of the graph). While here, the Australian dollar, the New Zealand dollar and the Japanese yen are most traded, yet they are often better to trade during the European and American sessions.

The reason is quite simple. According to the latest statistics of the BIS (Bank for International Settlements), the two largest Forex trading centers in the world, London and New York represented almost 60% of the trade turnover. While the share of New York with 18.9% in 2013 remained almost stable over the last 10 years, London could increase ist share significantly.

During the London session 40.9% of global transactions will be carried out in currency trading. For comparison: in 2013 Singapour got 5.7%, Tokyo 5.6%, and Hong Kong 4.1%.

Naturally, this has far-reaching consequences for forex scalpers. It is undisputed that the London session represents the most important hours of trading in international currency trading. As a trader, here you will find the best liquidity in all traded currency pairs.

You can expect at this time the best executions and the smallest spreads, which is of course for scalpers of extraordinary importance. Slippage is very limited at this time, which can not always be said of the Asian session.

However, experience shows that the volatility starts to increase already 1 hour before London open. This means for example, that breakout strategies succeed best at this time.

Due to the increased volatility at the beginning of the US session breakout strategies could be succesful too. Attention here! Trends of the European trading session can either be confirmed (trend following) or be turned abruptly (reversals). This is a consequence of expected economic data from the USA (usually at 08.30 EST, or 13.30 GMT).

Figure 5 also shows that the volatility towards the end of the London session (11.00 EST, 16.00 GMT) decreases, then remains at a low level during the the rest of the New York session and the Asian session. But this also has its advantages. Especially traders whose strategies are based on range markets, should prefer this quieter times. The probability that supports and resistances hold are significant higher here.


## B. For Index Trader

In the premarket (8:00 to 09:00 EST and GMT) all important news or information of the previous night is assimilated in the stock index futures which can lead to increased volatility. These are for traders in Europe often the "presettings" of Tokyo or China, but also those of the coming US markets. For American Traders the sentiment of the european trading session is important. If the sentiment is "good" the indices will generally start in positive territory. If the sentiment is bad more minus signs are to be expected.

This applies in principle to all stock markets and their indexes and futures. The Premarket is recommended therefore only really for experienced traders. During the assimilation-process of the new information a trend direction is specified, which is often retained for the rest of the day. Therefore, It can be lucrative to trade trendfollowing price patterns.

Often the high or low of the day occurs in the first hour of trading on the stock markets, (09:00 to 10:00 a.m.), but that's not always the case. On typical trend days you new highs or lows will occur after the first trading hour.

The best time to trade European indices such as the FTSE 100, DAX, CAC40 and the Eurostoxx50, is the morning session. From 13.00 (GMT) American traders come into the market bringing their own ideas, which can consistently reverse the trends of the European morning. As an Europe based trader I prefer to trade in the morning the European indices and in the afternoon the American indices.

In my experience American traders are more independent from the european session, allthough many of them do like to trade the DAX or other european indices. In general american markets are the most independent of all, wheras european markets tend to follow the American markets in the (european) afternoon. Nevertheless, if european indices are in the red, the premarket US futures will follow this direction first. But by the New York open everything can change quite soon.

### C. For oil traders

Oil futures are traded almost around the clock, but the most effective way to trade crude, is if the trader focuses on the so-called Prime Time. This is 08:50 -10:30 EST (or 13.50 - 15.30 GMT). In this hour and a half the best trading results are obtained, which was proved by statistical evaluations of trader results.

It is however crucial, that the trader avoids the first minute of the New York open. In this moment the "Pit"opens. You can often expected erratic movements, especially because pre-market information and new orders have to be processed.

An exception often forms the Wednesday when the Crude Inventories (Oil Market Report) will be published. These come at 10.30 EST (15.30 GMT). Traders should better wait on the publication. The hour thereafter is usually better to trade.

# 4. Why Fast Scalping is better than a few well-considered trades

We now come to the gist of this 4th part of „Scalping is fun!" I want to discuss here the main reasons why traders who "do everything right" yet fail.

Plane the Trade and trade the plan. It sounds so obvious and you read it in every other book on trading. The trader should prepare his transactions carefully after a thorough analysis of the charts. It's like if you would give a soccer team the advice: "In the first 90 minutes of the game you should study the behavior of the other team before shooting at the goal."

Because it sounds so convincing and because this process in many professions is actually the better way, this maxim was transmitted on trading. Of course, the construction of a house or the construction of a new car should be carried out according to rational criteria and in a carefully prepared plan.

The wrong conclusion on the trading happens because many are of the opinion that one should design a trading strategy like constructing a machine. The only problem is that stock courses simply do not behave like the individual parts of a machine. If you know the laws of mechanics, you can bend or sawing metal parts as you need it for your workpiece.

Once we enter the trading field however, we find ourselves in a world that is no longer manageable or controllable. Imagine, you would live in a city where streets, squares, houses and trees are not located in the same place as yesterday so that you could refer briefly after some familiarization.

You get up every morning and the street in which you live has changed completely overnight, the crossing is no longer where you would otherwise always turn right. And all other roads, buildings, gas stations, shopping centers are located every morning in a different place, you would have to find yet.

A surreal imagination? But this is what really happens when you enter the stock market. It is a totally insane world that seemingly exists without rules and rational laws. Your experience and knowledge of yesterday will not help you today, why such a thing as technical analysis is only of a very limited use.

Profound adepts of technical analysis also state that the known pattern as continuation patterns or reversal patterns in many cases barely work nowadays. Why? Everybody knows those patterns today. So you no longer have an advantage if you think you recognize a certain pattern on a chart. Often the exact opposite happens from what you would expect.

The same applies to the remainder of the available instruments of technical analysis such as indicators or oscillators or what that engineer brain else has invented. The look and feel of these instruments are based, without exception, on data from the past. So, they say nothing about the current events in the market and certainly nothing about the future.

All the analysis and their "confirmation" by the indicators is basically only there for the need for security of the human psyche. So no harm is meant, unfortunately they do not help. Uncertainty remains because insecurity is truly the essence of the stock market.

And this whole equipment is basically just there to determine entries. It's always about this one thing:

entries, entries and entries. This is also the most common question I hear: "Dear Heiken Ashi Trader, tell me now at last, where I need to get in."

The point is: me too, I do not know. Also, I can not predict the future, because, after all, this is the real question that is asked. The whole trading industry tries to satisfy the answer to this question. And it does it in an almost ingenious way and makes good money with it.

So, if I know, that nobody and no system or analysis can assist me in deciding whether to buy or sell something, what criterion should I use after all?

My answer is: try to develop an more experimental relationship with the financial markets. And be ready at any time to revise your decision (to close the position, or even to do the opposite, from what you have just thought (reverse position)).

I know, that for many people, this kind of "flexibility" causes anxiety and sometimes prevent them therefore to ever execute a trade at the stock exchange.

Try to run your trading as if you were actually getting off an airplane and walk around in a foreign city you completely ignore. Do you not go around there with a curious look? Do you not want to know which beauty or maybe surprises this city has to offer?

I really do not know if the next trade will bring a profit or a loss to me. I can only try. And that's really the difference between the art of engineering and trading. When trading you always remain an amateur, no matter how many decades 'experience' you have, sorry.

Experience in trading rather refers more to the handling of the stop management. A good trader has developed a kind of inner protective mechanism protecting him against excessive losses. Through constant repetition and practice of the stop-management complex patterns have emerged in his brain. They are series of interlocking neurons that carry a specific habit.

These habits make the difference between an experienced and an inexperienced trader. It's not about the knowledge to entries, and certainly not about any secret knowledge that could predict the courses.

Yet, these new habits have to be practiced. Experience shows, that it takes time and a lot of repetition to have these patterns formed.

It is known, that the NASA space shuttle consumes in the first few minutes after the start more fuel than during the rest of the flight. Why is this so? At the start, the Space Shuttle needs most of its energy in order to break away from the forces of gravity. Once in space, and free of the gravitational pull of the earth, the shuttle can hold momentum and fly as if it had no resistance.

That is exactly the difficulty of a beginner in the stock market. First, he needs an enormous amount of energy in order to acquire a small number of good habits. He needs to invest a lot of time and energy in order to move away from the gravity of human nature, so that he can move freely and confidently in the cosmos of the stock market.

That's the reason why I find speed more important than perfection. Therefore, beginners should simply start without hesitation and execute regular trades. By this their brains learns also to think quickly and react like the stock market. Once you get momentum as a scalper, you are hardly to stop.

That's why scalpers should also focus on those times when volatility is highest. Usually this is after important economic news and during the peak hours of trading.

The chance that a scalper generates "flow" at these times is much higher than during the off-hours. Flow is a sequence of actions that you perform with the necessary discipline and joy in doing. Trading success follows from the ease of doing. That's why it is so important that the scalper acts only at the times, in which the movements are clear and unambiguous. The fun turns eventually by itself, and consequently the success.

My formula for success is therefore: **Flow - Fun - success!**

According to the inventor of the term "flow", the American psychologist Mihaly Csikszentmihalyi, the occurrence of flow-feelings causes clear objectives, a full focus on the doing, the sense of control of the activitie, the conformity of requirement and ability beyond fear or boredom in apparent ease.

He stresses, that it is important that the work is done playfully. The man in the flow makes his work creatively and artistically. But it is also crucial that he can let go of the expectation of success. He should be free from fear and worry.

This is exactly what happens, when a scalper who is scalping his market in a focused way. He does not expect, he is free from fear and acts independently of profit and loss. He does it quickly, concentrated and without preconceived ideas in which direction the market will go in the next few seconds or minutes.

Flow is therefore more of a state and not a technique. In order to experience flow, all distractions must be eliminated. These therefore include extensive analyzes and the usual pondering over the market. A trader in flow is thus completely in the matter, as if it was only thing that exists.

Therefore, somebody, who is in flow has the feeling, that he forgets everything around him and that everything "disappears" around him. In flow times disappears or gets carried away.

Flow is not restricted to trading. It can occur in principle in any kind of activity, be it so easy. Many sportsmen know this very well. Skiers, sailors, but also soccer players and tennis players have this experience.

Closer to trading are the (now professional) successful players of computer games. These people report of flow experiences by providing the player fast consecutive tasks which may challenge him, however can be solved successfully with high probability.

All artistic activities are hardly conceivable without flow. Of course the musicians know this, but also painters and sculptors. And probably the clearest expression of flow can be observed in a dancing couple that floats over the parquet seemingly effortlessly to the sounds of music.

For the scalper, however, this does not mean that he will lose the respect of the market. On the contrary. Scalper belong to the category of traders, who probably developed the greatest respect for the market, because they know: everything can happen at any time in the market. And to be in the flow, means that the scalper is able to respond adequately.

# 5. Discipline is easier in flow

It is unfortunately true: Trading contradicts the whole of human nature. It runs completely contrary to what has been taught to us in the course of life. Starting with the "I want to be and must be right!" Until switching into the „hope mode" once a posiiton has gone into the red. The market eventually could turn..

The more time a trader begrudge, to think about what to do with a loss position, the sooner does the brooding and thinking about takes the upper hand. The consequences are often extremely desastrous for the account.

So, as soon as the "head" takes the rule in trading, a rebellious little devil appeares that in no case wants to close losing positions.

Of course, arguments can always be found. Here are some classic examples:

"On the resistance the market could turn back."

"He needs to go until the support 2 and then he starts to rise again."

"It is impossible, that the market can rise that far, it has already twice overbought the normal ATR."

"Such exaggerated prices are always corrected."

"The market overreacted just. Its only a matter of time until it returns. "

"The market always turned back rotated at this level. It can not last much longer, because the RSI is completely in the overbought area. "

"According to my calculations, the market has completely exhausted the Fibonacci Extension."

As you can see, the trader's arguments do not rule out why something should be different than it actually is. The refusal to recognize facts is absolutely typical for the traders who "only execute well considered trades" or "only trade on the basis of crystal-clear setups."

That all this simply not exist and are pure imaginations of the brain, this type of trader does not want to admit easily. That "the market" is a chaotic and totally unpredictable entity, which can turn the direction of 180 degrees at any time, is overlooked knowingly. This trader wants to get this monster under control and wrest away from him with all his strength his secret.

He overlooks the fact that he wants to get to grips something with a totally unsuitable instrument: the rational thinking, based on logical conclusions argumentative part of our brain.

As stated above, this part is the right place when it comes to constructing a new machine, to develop a software, or to build a house. Nobody will want to doubt this seriously.

When it comes to trade such a chaotic structure as the forex market or a stock index this part of the human mind failes completely. It is only logical that the rational mind is here in the search for "principles", recurring „patterns" that are "tradable" and "have a high statistical probability of success."

And the technical analysis has found a strong distribution among retail investors in the past 20 years, serving this need, of course, perfectly. Before that it was the fundamental analysis that has stimulated to buy or sell decisions. Now the trader refers to the charting technic as an instrument with which he can "read" and "interpret" the markets.

I do not want to belittle the merits of Technical Analysis here. Also, I have traded on the basis of Technicals myself for years. Yet, I never made any money with it.

But, the trader who enters into the venture to happyly and carefree ride the waves, as the chart draws him in front of his eyes, has at least a chance to react now and then adequately to market developments.

Because, that is what trading ultimately is: Responding to what the market has to say to me now in this moment.

On good days, such a trader can actually get into some kind of "flow" in which he may have the impression at least temporarily to act "in accordance with the market".

This method, which I have been practicing for years is certainly not infallible. Again, there will be loss days or market phases in which it does not work well.

Nevertheless, these scalping method can bring a lot of joy and a lot of gain with increasing practice and experience to the traders. And, as I said more often, if it is not fun, you should just stop scalping.

One should actually go to these high market phases (usually after the release of important market data) and then try to scalp with courage and chutzpah.

It is exactly in the quick movements that produce clear buy and sell waves in which I make the most gains. My personal record is 28 winners in succession.

If then first losses show up, this is often a first warning sign that either I get tired, or the market. It may be a temporary slowdown of momentum. It could also be that the dynamics simply decreases and the market movements are no longer so easily to trade. Mostly this is the best time to take a break or even stop altogether for the day.

But the fact is that the aforementioned discipline problems occur much less while scalping fast and dynamic than with the "well chosen" trades.

A trader who is in full flow, knows in the moment what to do when the market suddenly turns against him. He closes his position without question, whether in profit or loss. He acts decisively and without hesitation. Fast scalping promotes the rapid closing of losing positions and also the quick takeaway from accrued profits, which is equally important.

My experience is that the two basic problems of trading - fear and greed - are better controlled here. With this method the trader simply has no time to ponder.

That is why I recommend trading with one-click orders using this method. If the trader has to open a folder and enter a number, while the market runs against his position every second, he will lose important points or pips.

If the trader works with one-click orders, he is with just a single click of the mouse button out of the market and he should when he is are on the wrong side of the trade.

# 6. Warning and Control Instruments

Now that you know how to scalp and especially when, "only" the task remains to do it. Easy to say, because what is easy to do, is well known, is easy to do not. The full potential of trading and scalpings truly does not lie in the complexity of the task. The magic lies in the daily repetition of this task.

As I have tried to show in the third book of this series "How do I rate my trading results?" based on the trading results of a single trader, the full potential of scalping shows up only gradually. It's by the daily routine that the trader eventually can become master of his craft. This also means that has to learn to listen to certain warning signs of the market, which will tell him when to stop.

Scalpen in Forex can basically be done around the clock, but I hope this book has shown, that there are certain hours when this can be done much more successful than in others. If the trader scalps in boring and slow markets rather than in fast, dynamic markets, he also will slow down and his trades will need time to reach their target.

By contrast, at first there is no objection against this. The trader just need to know that a different brain activity begins as soon as he has to wait for his results. He will be distracted and not focused to track his trades as they should. Therefore, a sudden slowdown is mostly a clear sign that he should stop scalping.

Yet, the other extreme also exists. It happens rarely, thank God, but there were times in the last 15 years times when volatility took so crazy dimensions that was it was no longer reasonable to think of trading or scalping.

During the days of the euro crisis of 2011 I have seen the EUR/USD crash 50 pips sometimes within one second! It is clear that a trader will have a hard time to keep his risk management consistently in such markets. It would be better when he stops scalping whenever he observes such crazy movements. And if ever he can not stop, he should continue with only a fraction of his normal position size.

The best and most important control tool for your trading business is your account. Nothing gives you a better feedback than your account balance. It is merciless and wont never ly. Your account tells you openly, whether your work is successful or not.

That's why I say: A trader is not trading the market, he is trading his account. Maybe the reader may will find this statement perhaps absurd, because he might think that trading has something to do with charts and strategies.

That is certainly the case, but there is no more important monitoring tool in your business as the equity curve of the trader. It shows the progress of the account balance from hour to hour and from day to day. Studying this curve, its history, the size of the drawdowns and how long the trader needs to recover from these drawdowns. A better feedback can not exist.

This is also true for an intraday view. If after 20 trades where the trader has made a tidy profit, he suddenly find out that increasingly losers occur, he should at least take a break, if not stop altogether. He should get up, go out into the fresh air and think about whether the market is worth it that he devotes his precious time.

If he notices that the price movements meet his criteria for scalping again, he can continue. But should he find out that the market has become slow, is going sideways or indecisive movements makes it difficult to trade, he should better stop. Maybe the trader has the best part of the day behind. Tomorrow he can come back.

What is written down here easily, is much more difficult to carry out in practice. I know that some traders are obsessed about the markets and can not stop despite clear warning signs.

They simply continue to trade, because they can not leave it. They ignore all the warning signs. The consequences can be imagined. It happens quite often that these traders los all accrued profits of the day and even produce losses.

I can not repeat it often enough. Successful traders know especially when you should not trade. Perhaps this is the most important trading rule at all.

Of course a beginner does not know this. H e has not yet learned to distinguish between good markets (for his strategy) and bad markets. But it's part of the training. He has to learn it if he ever wants to succeed in trading.

If he can not stop, he should at least reduce his position size, if it is not going well. Then the damage that he aligns to his account is restricted.

My longest loss series in scalping were 15 losing trades. You read that right: fifteen losers in succession without a single winning trade between. The reader might think, that is statistically not possible. However, it is possible, I did it.

It is just as possible as the above-mentioned series of 28 winning trades in succession with my scalping method. Admittedly, the market was extremely well that day. The waves on the in 1-minute Heikin Ashi Chart were as clear and easy to see, so that each trade was a hit.

After the 29th trade (which of course was a loser) I stopped. I even turned off the PC, because I felt instinctively: "Now you can only mess it up by yourself."

Unfortunately, I was not always that wise. I have violated my own rule too often, to quit as soon as I start to lose. But that does not not mean that the rule is not valid.

We are and remain human. We make mistakes and will make mistakes in the future.

The trader should not be too severe with himself if he has violated his own rules. He will do it and will do it again. Nothing is set in stone in trading.

Nevertheless, the warning signs of a trader are vital if he wants to build this business successfully and one day make a living of it.

If he learns to respect the warning signs, which gives him the market and his account, he will become guaranteed a better trader over time. And that will be reflected on his account balance.

# 7. Be aggressive when you win and defensive when you lose

We have now compiled important success factors. We now know when we should scalp and especially when not. We have found out, that discipline is easier to achieve with rapid markets rather than in boring sideways markets. Finally, we have met important warning and control instruments such as drawdowns and sudden losses.

It now remains to address the key success factor of all: the active management of the position size.

Traders have basically three freedoms: they have to decide what to buy (this is the field of fundamental analysis). They have to decide when to buy (this is the field of technical analysis). After all, they have to decide how much they buy (this is the field of active money management).

In my eyes, when scalping, the how much should not be pending from any randomly chosen position sizing algorithm. Fixed rules like "never risking more than 1% of your capital per transaction" are certainly useful when one is at the beginning. First, ist about having any risk management control at all. But this rule can be a hindrance in the long run, if you really want to run a dynamic position management.

And this has a lot to do with what has been said. Once a scalper mastered the timing, then he also knows when to stop scalping, and then he can begin to adjust his position size to market events.

The scalper trade with larger positions when things are going well and reduce the position, if not.

What sounds simple is not easy to implement in practice. What to do if the trader has a winning series and instead of the customary two lots he scalps now up 5 lots in the Forex market. And suddenly he produces two losers? Should he continue to scalp with 5 lots?

I am always keen that in complex decision-making processes rules should be established that are as simple and clear as possible. When the trader is scalping he simply does not have the time to make big thoughts about his money management.

So also here: Keep it simple! If he has two losing trades in succession, he should at least halve the position size. So if has been scalping with 5 lots, this means that now he should scalp with 2 lots until he is successful again.

Incidentally, 2 losing trades in succession are also a kind of warning. If the trader scalps much, two losing trades are of course not unusual. Still, it's a sign that his system currently is not so well in keeping with the market situation. So, he should be more defensive in this situation.

Has he just realized 7 winning trades in succession, this is surely a sign that it is running well and his method suits well with the current market. Here he can be more aggressive and scalp with larger positions.

Good scalper know when it's time to turn on the turbo concerning their position size and when not. There are days when you can make $ 10,000 or more on the stock exchange. And there are days when you can be satisfied with a gain of $ 250 Euro.

The aim of this e-books is to make the trader aware of the great trading days. In my eyes, here is one of the true trader secrets. Good traders know when the roast is served. They also know when it is usually not worthwhile to go to dinner.

And the very experienced ones have learned only to appear on feast days and elsewhere "to sit on their hands".

This is certainly very difficult and requires a lot of discipline. Nevertheless, it is worth. The beginning trader will eventually realize that the results of trading occur asymmetrically. Profits are not even uniformly distributed over 20 trading days per month like in a 9 to 5 job.

Unfortunately, I have understood this myself very late. I have always understood trading as a kind of trading office job, that is been operated as something that you should do disciplined on a daily basis. But it is not working that way. If the trader trades and scalps in this way, the results will be mediocre at best (as in almost all office jobs ...).

The whole art of trading consists in the ability to actually apply the knowledge on the stock market festive days (or hours). If the trader succeed, only risking his money, when it is really worth and then right to slog away, not fiddling around, the chance that he will be among the 5% winners in the stock market is very large.

Parent, the position size also depends on his current mental being. Should he be the last few days not in a very good mood, running somewhat tempered by the area, then he should not try to compensate his bad mood by an aggressive approach on the stock market.

I know that this temptation exists, but it is not really a sign of professionalism, if the trader tries to compensate his current status in private life by an aggressive style. Mostly this is not going to work out.

A good scalper is therefore also a good seismograph of himself. He knows exactly when to be active and when he can act with bigger positions in the market. And he also knows intuitively when this is not the case. If his assessment is sometimes wrong, then his account balance will quickly disabuse him.

Each trader also has natural limits. There are traders who already experience a sense of danger and overwork when they trade more than 1 standard lot. Whether they will be able to one day overcome this limit, depends on their ability to leave their comfort zone.

I knew a very good trader who could never trade more than 2 contracts in the E-mini and the mini-Dow futures, although he had decades of experience and came almost every day with profits from the market.

I told him he could trade a lot more contracts and thus earn more money. But he would not. Two contracts were his natural limit. This trader knew his own comfort zone very well and respected it.

The opposite,unfortunately, exist also. There are quite a lot traders who are totally overleveraged in the market. Some that I've met, risked more than 10% of their trading capital per transaction. I knew it was only a matter of time until they would realize their 10 sequentially losing trades. Game over!

Trading and scalping can be incredibly lucrative for disciplined individuals who overcome their natural fear limits with increasing experience. I hope, with this eBook I could give some impetus to this success.

I wish you, dear reader, good luck with your trading activities!

Heikin Ashi Trader

# More books by Heikin Ashi Trader

**How to start a Trading Business with $500**

Many new traders have little capital available in the beginning, but this is not an obstacle to starting a trading career anyway.

However, this book is not about how to grow a $500 account into a $500,000 account. It is precisely these exaggerated return expectations that bring most beginners to failure.

Instead, the author shows, in a realistic way, how you can become a full-time trader in spite of limited start-up capital. This applies both for traders who want to remain private, as well as for those who want to eventually trade customer funds.

This book shows step by step how to do it. In addition, there is a concrete action plan for each step. Anyone can be a trader in principle, if he or she is willing to learn how this business works.

# Contents

# About the Author

Heikin Ashi Trader is recognized worldwide as the specialist in scalping with the Heikin Ashi chart. He has been trading this way for 19 years. He traded for a hedge fund and then went into business for himself as a trader. His scalping book "Scalping is Fun!" is an international bestseller and has been sold more than 30,000 times. You can find more information about his scalping method on his website www.heikinashitrader.net

# Imprint

Texts: © Copyright by Heikin Ashi Trader
Swiss Post Box 106287
Zürcher Strasse 161
CH-8010 Zürich
Switzerland

www.ingramcontent.com/pod-product-compliance
Lightning Source LLC
Chambersburg PA
CBHW070421190526
45169CB00003B/1358